AF599564

ENGLAND

Tracy Vonder Brink

TABLE OF CONTENTS

A Crabtree Seedlings Book

School-to-Home Support for Caregivers and Teachers

This book helps children grow by letting them practice reading. Here are a few guiding questions to help the reader with building his or her comprehension skills. Possible answers appear here in red.

Before Reading:

- What do I think this book is about?
    - *I think this book is about England.*
    - *I think this book is about the people of England.*

- What do I want to learn about this topic?
    - *I want to learn where England is.*
    - *I want to learn about the weather in England.*

During Reading:

- I wonder why...
    - *I wonder why the White Cliffs are white.*
    - *I wonder why Stonehenge was built.*

What have I learned so far?

- *I have learned that England is part of Europe.*
- *I have learned that Westminster Abbey is more than 700 years old.*

After Reading:

- What details did I learn about this topic?
    - *I have learned that the Tower of London is a castle.*
    - *I have learned that the British Museum is one of the largest museums in the world.*

- Read the book again and look for the vocabulary words.
    - *I see the word* ***capital*** *on page 4, and the word* ***statues*** *on page 10. The other glossary words are on pages 22 and 23.*

England is a country.

It is part of **Europe**.

England is on an island.

London is England's **capital**.
A river flows through the city.
It is called the River Thames.

Most people in England speak English.

London has many famous buildings.

The Tower of London is a castle.

Many people visit it.

ENTRY TO THE TRAITORS' GATE

Westminster Abbey is a church. It is more than 700 years old.

The British Museum is one of the largest museums in the world.

It holds **statues**, paintings, and more.

Millions of people visit the British Museum every year.

Oxford is near London. It has a famous **university**. Students from all over the world learn there.

Some parts of England's countryside have low, green hills.

Pretty villages are found in the Cotswolds **region**.

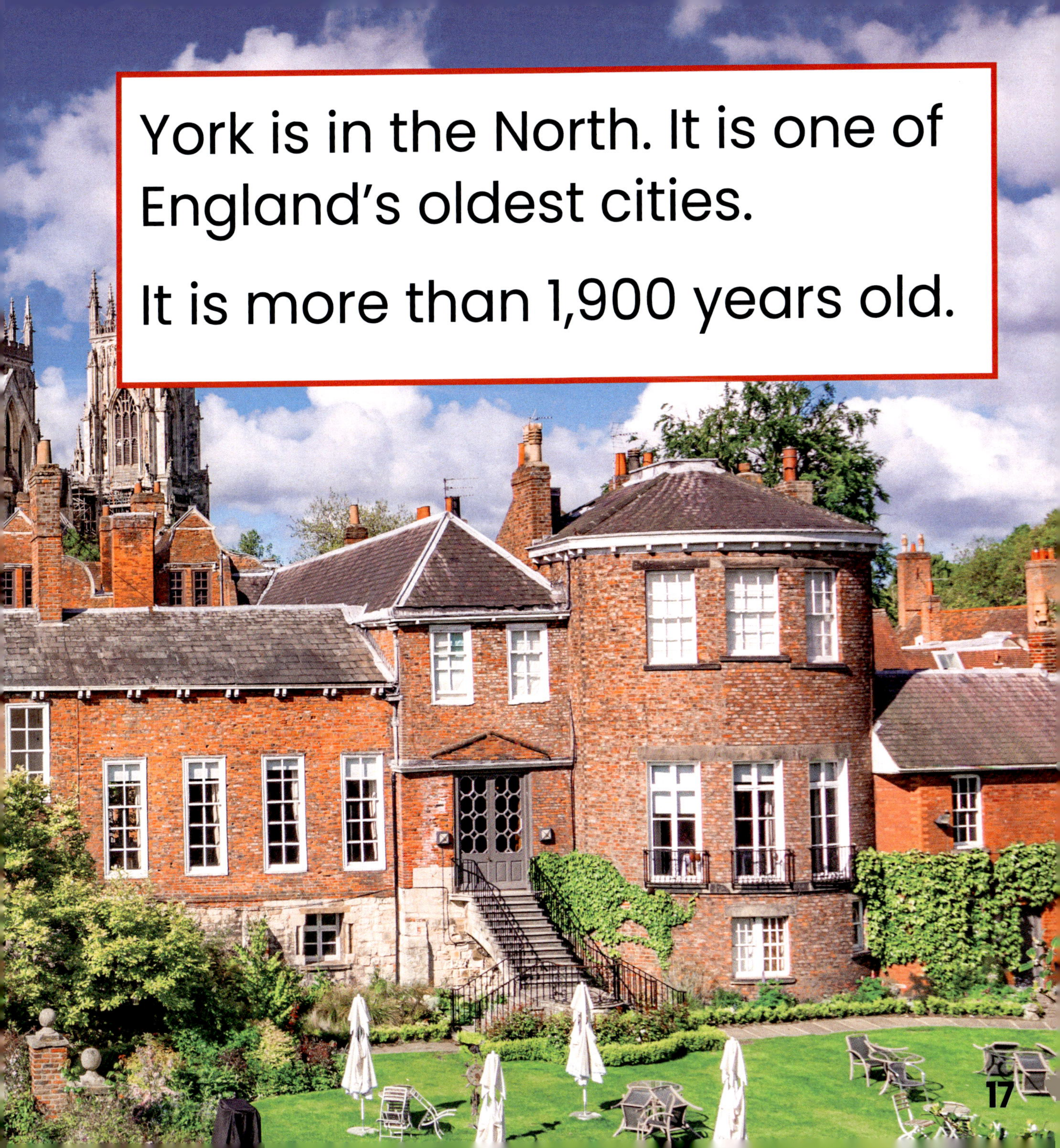

York is in the North. It is one of England's oldest cities.

It is more than 1,900 years old.

The White Cliffs of Dover are on England's **coast**.

They are white because they are made of chalk.

This circle of stones is called Stonehenge.

Stonehenge was built about 5,000 years ago.

England has many places to visit!

Nobody knows exactly who built Stonehenge or why.

Glossary

capital (KAP-i-tl): The city where the government of a country or a state is located

coast (kohst): The land next to the ocean or sea

Europe (YOOR-up): The continent between the Atlantic Ocean and Asia

region (REE-juhn): A particular area of a state, country, or the world

statue: (STA-choo): A figure of a person or an animal made by an artist from a hard material such as metal or stone

university (yoo-nuh-VUR-suh-tee): A school of higher learning and research that a person can go to after high school

Index

About the Author

Tracy Vonder Brink

Tracy Vonder Brink loves to visit new places. She has visited England and enjoyed seeing London. She lives in Cincinnati, Ohio, with her husband, two daughters, and two rescue dogs.

Written by: Tracy Vonder Brink
Designed by: Niko Magaro
Series Development: James Earley
Proofreader: Melissa Boyce
Educational Consultant: Marie Lemke M.Ed.

Photographs: All images from Shutterstock

Crabtree Publishing

crabtreebooks.com 800-387-7650

Printed in the U.S.A./062024/CG20240201

Published in Canada
Crabtree Publishing
616 Welland Avenue
St. Catharines, Ontario
L2M 5V6

Published in the United States
Crabtree Publishing
347 Fifth Avenue
Suite 1402-145
New York, New York, 10016

Library and Archives Canada Cataloguing in Publication
Available at Library and Archives Canada

Library of Congress Cataloging-in-Publication Data
Available at the Library of Congress

Hardcover: 978-1-0398-4484-1
Paperback: 978-1-0398-4565-7
Ebook (pdf): 978-1-0398-4637-1
Epub: 978-1-0398-4707-1
Read-Along: 978-1-0398-4777-4
Audio: 978-1-0398-4847-4